E&L 19 (07/05)

Renfrewshire
Council

EDUCATION AND LEISURE SERVICES
LIBRARIES

Thank you for using _____
Library. Please return by the last date below. Renewals can be requested in person, by telephone or via our website www.renfrewshire.gov.uk/libraries

Bargarran 0141 812 2841	Bishopton 01505 862 136
Bridge of Weir 01505 612 220	Central 0141 887 3672
Elderslie 01505 322 055	Erskine 0141 812 5331
Ferguslie Park 0141 887 6404	Foxbar 01505 812 353
Gallowhill 0141 889 1195	Glenburn 0141 884 2874
Johnstone 01505 329 726	Library HQ 0141 840 3003
Linwood 01505 325 283	Lochwinnoch 01505 842 305
Mobiles 0141 889 1195	Ralston 0141 882 1879
Renfrew 0141 886 3433	Todholm 0141 887 3012
Toy Library 0141 884 8000	

The Collector's Book of

Badges & Emblems

of the

British Forces

1940

The Collector's Book of

Badges & Emblems

of the

British Forces

1940

Introduction by F. J. Wilkinson

Greenhill
Books

This edition of *The Collector's Book of Badges and Emblems
of the British Forces, 1940* first published 1988 by
Greenhill Books, Lionel Leventhal Limited,
Park House, 1 Russell Gardens, London NW11 9NN

British Library Cataloguing in Publication Data
The Collector's Book of Badges and Emblems
of the British Forces, 1940.
1. Great Britain, *Army* – Medals, Badges, Decorations, etc.
2. Armies – Commonwealth of Nations – Insignia
I. Badges and Emblems of the Services
355.1'4 UC535.G7

ISBN 0–947898–82-4

Publishing History
The Collector's Book of Badges and Emblems of the British Forces, 1940
was first published in book form in 1940 under the title *Badges and
Emblems of the Services* (N.A.G. Press Ltd., London). This edition
presents the content of the original volume, with the addition
of a new Introduction by F. J. Wilkinson.

Printed by Antony Rowe Limited,
Chippenham, Wiltshire

COLLECTING BADGES

Despite a very long national history of military success on every continent, the average British citizen has seldom had more than a passing interest in the armed forces. This was certainly true in 1939 when the Second World War broke out, but then the British Isles became one great military base with men in the uniform of many nations. There were servicemen from all over the mighty British Empire, from Canada, Australia, New Zealand, South Africa and India. There were also large numbers of Poles who had escaped after the defeat of their country by the Germans and were then continuing the struggle from Britain. In 1940 they were joined by similar exiles from Norway, Denmark, Belgium, Holland and France as their countries were occupied by the seemingly invincible German forces.

In these circumstances it became impossible not to be interested in the armed forces and their badges, and it was to meet the demand for information that a number of booklets, pamphlets and articles, both official and private, were published. However, very few of these publications survived, and original copies are scarce. This particular publication now being reprinted is complete for a key period – the start of the Second World War – and is of special interest, since its coverage is not limited to the armed forces alone but includes badges of various other wartime bodies such as the Civil Defence, Police, Fire and Nursing Services. In addition to identifying the numerous badges and rank insignia, the captions give a brief potted history of the various units.

Victory came to the Allies in 1945, and not surprisingly after five years of war there was a falling off of people's interest in anything to do with the military. Uniforms and badges were largely a thing of the past, reminders of a painful period. However a few retained their interest in cap badges and continued to collect and study them. Specimens were common, and there was little demand – a few pence would purchase the majority of common badges, and there was only limited interest in earlier examples. The hobby gradually attracted more dedicated enthusiasts who researched the subject and began to publish authoritative articles which, in turn, stimulated further interest and so increased the number of collectors. Several books were published and what had previously been mainly a small boys' hobby became adult and respectable. Specialist societies were formed and flourished.

As the demand for limited stocks of badges and emblems increased, prices began to rise. Inevitably the limited supply was enhanced by modern copies and then came that great problem: the restrike. Using original dies or new high-tech copying techniques, facsimile badges were struck; the quality of these replicas improved until it became difficult to tell the original from the restrike. Today it is difficult for even the most experienced collectors to be one hundred per cent certain as to which is the original and which the facsimile. If these restrikes are sold as copies, there is less of a problem. However there are unscrupulous dealers who sell them to innocent collectors as originals at prices commanded by genuine pieces.

In addition to the numerous cap badges, the armed forces have used at different periods a wide range of metal shoulder-titles, collar badges and cloth insignia. All are now keenly collected.

The general use of unit badges by the British Army began in the seventeenth century and developed apace during the eighteenth and nineteenth centuries. During the long history of the British Army there have been many changes in organisation, nomenclature and uniforms and the identification and dating of early badges is not easy. It is not unknown for some regiments to be ignorant of details of their earlier badges. Many regiments have worn a variety of badges, mostly with a common theme; the search for these variants adds to the interest of badge collecting, which has now become a popular hobby world-wide.

Today the collector is well catered for with several magazines carrying reliable articles and societies specialising in different aspects of the hobby. Many auction houses include badges in their sales of arms and armour, and antiques fairs devoted to arms, armour and militaria flourish across the country. Over the years a number of books have been published, and the collector will find the books mentioned in the bibliography at the end of this Introduction of value.

However, despite all these advantages, the collector needs to be very careful indeed, for ignorance and greed have led to copies and restrikes appearing in growing numbers. Dealers should be prepared to give a guarantee that any item is genuine but the value of this guarantee is in proportion to the vendor's degree of expertise. A good and knowledgeable dealer is to be valued! The collector should take every opportunity to examine badges – one of the best methods is to join a club or society, for the majority of members are always ready to share their expertise. Experience is the only real safeguard against bad purchases but even with all the expertise mistakes can still be made!

Badge collecting is a fascinating hobby and, by comparison, still a fairly cheap one. Very rare badges may cost hundreds of pounds, but the vast majority can be acquired for no more than a few pounds. Badges offer the collector a contact with history and may encourage the exploration of many side-avenues such as regimental details, the study of such topics as uniforms, campaign histories, medals, biographies of people connected with the various units, weapons and equipment. In addition to all these academic pastimes, this is a hobby that affords its followers hours of quiet enjoyment.

F. J. WILKINSON, 1988

BIBLIOGRAPHY

Bloomer, W. and Bloomer K. *Badges Of The Highland And Lowland Regiments*, London, 1982.

Carman, W. Y., *Glengarry Badges Of The British Line Regiments To 1881*, London, 1973.

Churchill, C. and Westlake, R., *British Army Collar Badges, 1881 To The Present* London 1986.

Cox, R. H., *Military Badges Of The British Empire*, London, 1982.

Gaylor, J., *Military Badge Collecting*, London. 1977.

Kipling, A. L. and King, H. L., *Head-Dress Badges Of The British Army*, London, Vol. 1 1978, Vol. 2 1979.

May, M., Carman, W. and Tanner, J., *Badges And Insignia Of The British Armed Services*, London, 1974.

Parkyn, H. G., *Shoulder Belt Plates And Buttons*, London, 1987 (reprint).

Rosignoli, G., *Army Badges And Insignia Of World War 2*, London, Vol. 1 1972, Vol. 2 1975.

Wilkinson, F., *Badges Of The British Army 1820 To The Present*, London, 1987.

The Collector's Book of

Badges & Emblems

of the

British Forces
1940

ACKNOWLEDGEMENT

Grateful acknowledgement for assistance in the original 1940 compilation of this book, and facilities for the reproduction of badges was made to the authorities of the Admiralty, War Office, Air Ministry, India Offices, Imperial War Museum, Offices of the High Commissioners for Canada, South Africa, Australia, the Commissioner of Police, Officials of the various Nursing and Civil Defence and other bodies, and to Messrs. J. R. Gaunt and Son, Ltd., Messrs. Simpson (Piccadilly) Ltd., the Goldsmiths Journal and others by whose generous aid and co-operation this book has been made possible.

BADGE OF
THE BRITISH ARMY

Introduced in 1939. Based on a design by Captain Oakes-Jones, Honorary Adviser, Military Display, to the War Office for a window in Ypres Cathedral in memory of King Albert of the Belgians. The badge is the window design simplified.

ROYAL NAVY
(Officer's Cap Badge)

THE SENIOR service. First naval victories won by Alfred the Great's fleet. England's sea power began under Henry VII and later saved her from invasion by Napoleon's armies. Officer's cap badge of the Royal Navy is the crown, the "foul anchor" and the wreath. Rank is indicated by the oak leaves on the peak of the cap. Cap badges were officially instituted in 1846. Women's R.N. Service Officer's badge is similar, but oak leaves are blue instead of gold.

ROYAL MARINES

FIRST MARINE regiment, the Duke of York and Albany's Regiment of Foot was formed in 1664. Are trained as soldiers for service with the Fleet. Badge: The the globe, granted in 1827, surrounded by a laurel wreath awarded in 1761. Motto is *Per Mare Per Terram.*

FLEET AIR ARM
(Pilot's Wings)

BADGE OF members of the Fleet Air Arm; worn by officers of the Fleet Air Arm on their sleeves. Since May, 1939, has been under the Admiralty, and the naval uniform is worn by personnel. Formed in April, 1924.

MERCHANT NAVY
(Cap Badge)

CAP BADGE of officers and cadets above rank of petty officer is the naval crown, a silver anchor on a red cushion and a wreath. The design of the crown dates back to the middle of the eighteenth century and is based on the design of the Roman naval crowns.

EMBLEMS OF NAVAL RANKS

ADMIRAL OF THE FLEET
(A.D.C. to the King)

ADMIRAL

VICE-ADMIRAL

REAR-ADMIRAL or COMMODORE
(1st Class)

COMMODORE
(2nd Class)

CAPTAIN

COMMANDER

LIEUTENANT-COMMANDER

LIEUTENANT

SUB-LIEUTENANT

WARRANT OFFICER
(Thinner Stripe)

MIDSHIPMAN or NAVAL CADET

FLEET AIR ARM

LIEUTENANT R.N.R.

LIEUTENANT R.N.V.R.

NAVAL CADET LAPEL

EMBLEMS OF ARMY & R.M. RANKS

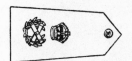

FIELD-MARSHAL

GENERAL

LIEUTENANT-
GENERAL

MAJOR-GENERAL

BRIGADIER

COLONEL

LIEUTENANT-
COLONEL

MAJOR

CAPTAIN

LIEUTENANT

2nd LIEUTENANT

ROYAL MARINES
(Emblems as Army with
addition of R.M.)

THE LIFE GUARDS

THE OLDEST cavalry regiment of the British Army dates back to 1660. One of the few regiments to have survived mechanisation. Part of the Household Cavalry, attendant upon the King and Queen. Badge: The Royal Cipher; Motto: *Honi Soit qui mal y Pense.*

ROYAL HORSE GUARDS
(The Blues)

PART OF the Household Cavalry. Early name the Oxford Blues, after its Colonel, the Earl of Oxford. History of the Blues goes back to the time of Cromwell. Badge: The Royal Cipher; Motto: *Honi Soit qui mal y Pense.*

1st KING'S DRAGOON GUARDS

FOUNDED 1685. Became an armoured car unit in 1938. Badge: Imperial Eagle of Austria, bestowed when the Emperor of Austria was Colonel-in-Chief between 1896 and 1914; removed in 1914, it was restored in 1938; Mottoes: *Honi Soit qui mal y Pense; Dieu et mon Droit.*

THE QUEEN'S BAYS
(2nd Dragoon Guards)

A UNIT of the Royal Armoured Corps; mechanised 1936-37. Badge: Laurel Wreath and Crown. Colonel-in-Chief H.M. The Queen; Mottoes: *Honi Soit qui mal y Pense; Pro Rege et Patria.*

For Meanings of Mottoes, See pages 60 and 61.

3rd CARABINIERS
(Prince of Wales's Dragoon Guards)

CONSISTS OF two regiments amalgamated in 1922, the 3rd (Prince of Wales's Dragoon Guards) and the 6th Dragoon Guards (Carabiniers). Now mechanised. Badge : Prince of Wales's Feathers and crossed carbines ; Motto : *Ich Dien.*

4th/7th ROYAL DRAGOON GUARDS

IN 1922 the 4th (Royal Irish) Dragoon Guards and the 7th (Princess Royal's) Dragoon Guards were merged into the 4th/7th Dragoon Guards ; now mechanised. The title *Royal* restored in 1936. Badge : Coronet backed against the Star of the Order of St. Patrick. Motto : *Quis Separabit ?*

5th ROYAL INNISKILLING DRAGOON GUARDS

MERGED FROM two separate bodies in 1922 into the 5th Inniskilling Dragoon Guards ; now mechanised. The title *Royal* was given to commemorate the Silver Jubilee in 1935. Badge : Monogram and Crown ; Motto : *Vestigia nulla retrorsum.*

1st THE ROYAL DRAGOONS

ONE OF the two Dragoon Regiments of the Army and both still have their horses. The regiment was formed in 1661. Badge : The Royal Crest ; Motto : *Spectemur Agendo.* Colonel-in-Chief : H.M. The King.

THE ROYAL SCOTS GREYS

THE SECOND dragoon regiment of the Army which retains its horses. Formed 1681; first mounted on greys 1700. Badge: An eagle, commemorating the capture of the Eagle Standard of the French 45th Regiment at Waterloo. Second Badge: The White Horse of Hanover, worn on the back of the full dress bearskin. Colonel-in-Chief: H.M. The King. Among their mottoes is: *Second to None.*

3rd THE KING'S OWN HUSSARS

BRITISH HUSSARS introduced in 1806. This regiment was formed in 1685, and took its present name in 1861. Armoured car unit 1936. Badge: The White Horse of Hanover; Motto: *Nec aspera ferrent.*

4th QUEEN'S OWN HUSSARS

THE "FOURTH" bears its number on its badge; Motto: *Mente et Manu.* Formed in 1685, mechanised 1937. The last time it took part in a ceremony on its horses was at the Jubilee of King George V.

7th QUEEN'S OWN HUSSARS

FIRST FORMED in 1689 as "Cunningham's Dragoons." Badge: Monogram Q.O. ("Queen's Own"). Motto: *Honi Soit qui mal y Pense.*

10th ROYAL HUSSARS
(Prince of Wales's Own)

FORMED IN Hertfordshire in 1697; title " Royal " awarded for services in the Peninsular war ; mechanised 1936. Badge : the Prince of Wales's Feathers. Motto : *Ich Dien.* The Duke of Gloucester, Colonel-in-Chief, served in the regiment for 15 years.

11th HUSSARS
(Prince Albert's Own)

THE REGIMENT provided an escort for the Prince Consort when he arrived in this country. The first cavalry regiment to be mechanised; 1928. Badge : Crest, Prince Consort. Motto : *Treu und Fest.*

8th KING'S
ROYAL IRISH HUSSARS

FORMED IN Ireland in 1693 and became the King's Royal Irish Regiment of Light Dragoons, 1776 ; now mechanised. Badge : Irish Harp and Crown. Motto : *Pristinæ Virtutis Memores.*

9th QUEEN'S
ROYAL LANCERS

LANCERS WERE introduced into the British Army in 1816 ; the title of the regiment was given by William IV in honour of his Queen. Mechanised 1937. Badge : Crossed lances and the figure " 9."

12th ROYAL LANCERS
(Prince of Wales's)

FORMED IN 1697; became an armoured car unit in 1928. Badge : Crossed lances, the Prince of Wales's Feathers and regimental number ; Motto : *Ich Dien.*

13th/18th
ROYAL HUSSARS

THE 13TH Hussars and the 18th Queen Mary's Own Royal Hussars combined in 1922 to form one regiment ; now mechanised. Badge : Numbers 13 and 18, Monogram Q.M.O. Colonel-in-Chief : Queen Mary.

14th/20th HUSSARS

THE 14TH King's Hussars and the 20th Hussars, amalgamated 1922 ; the 14th were formed in 1697 and the 20th in 1759. Badge : The Prussian Eagle ; Motto : *Honi Soit qui mal y Pense.*

15th/19th THE KING'S
ROYAL HUSSARS

THE REGIMENT is a merger of 1922 of the 15th (The King's) Hussars and the 19th Queen Alexandra's Own Royal Hussars. Badge : Royal Crest ; Motto : *Merebimur.*

16th/5th LANCERS

17th/21st LANCERS

THE 16TH The Queen's Lancers and the 5th Royal Irish Lancers merged in 1922. The 16th was raised in 1759, was the first British regiment to fight with lances. The 5th was formed in 1689. Badge: Crossed lances and "16."

THE NICKNAME of the 17th Lancers (Duke of Cambridge's Own) is the "Death or Glory Boys." Merged with 21st Lancers (Empress of India's) in 1922. Badge: Skull and Cross-Bones. Motto: *Or Glory.*

THE SEAFORTH HIGHLANDERS
(Ross-shire Buffs, The Duke of Albany's)

THE ROYAL WILTSHIRE YEOMANRY
(Prince of Wales's Own)

FIRST AND Second battalions raised by the Earl of Seaforth in the eighteenth century. Tartan worn is that of the Mackenzies, although the Stuart tartan is carried on pipe ribbons. Badge: The stag's head, the crest of the Earl of Seaforth. Motto: *Cuidich'n Righ.*

FOUNDED IN Devizes in May 1794, becoming the Regiment of Wiltshire Yeomanry Cavalry in 1797. Received its title of "Royal" in 1830. Their battle honours include South Africa, Ypres, Somme, France and Flanders. Badge: The Prince of Wales's Plume. Motto: *Ich Dien.*

ROYAL REGIMENT OF ARTILLERY

Now consists of Field Artillery, Coast Defence Artillery, Anti-aircraft and some searchlight units. Last horse battery was mechanised in 1939. Badge: A gun. Mottoes: *Ubique* above and *Quo Fas et Gloria Ducunt* below.

HONOURABLE ARTILLERY COMPANY

Probably the oldest regiment in the world. Granted a charter in 1537 as a Guild of Archers and Hand Gunmen. Sole regiment to have its battle honours on its King's Colours only. Captain-General H.M. The King. Badge: A gun with the initials H.A.C. above. Motto: *Arma Pacis Fulcra.*

ROYAL MALTA ARTILLERY

A battle honour was won in Egypt in 1882. Badge: A gun backed by the Maltese Cross. Motto: *Tutela Bellicae Virtutis.*

CORPS OF ROYAL ENGINEERS

Founded in 1683. Its duties are many and involve bridge building, mining and planning defence works. Popular nickname "Sappers." Badge: Royal Cipher and Wreath. Motto: *Honi Soit qui mal y Pense.*

ROYAL CORPS ON SIGNALS

CREATED FROM the Royal Engineers after the 1914-1918 war to deal with army communications. Badge: Mercury, messenger of the gods, poised on a globe. Motto: *Certa Cito.*

ROYAL TANK REGIMENT

BECAME AN independent regiment after the 1914-18 war, in which it was known as the Royal Tank Corps. Assumed its present title recently. Badge: A tank encircled by a laurel wreath. Motto: Fear Naught. Colonel-in-Chief: H.M. The King.

NORTH IRISH HORSE

NOW MECHANISED. Battle honours gained in the last war include those won during the retreat from Mons and at the Marne, Armentiere, Bapaume, Cambrai and Selle. Badge: Irish Harp and Crown.

THE RIFLE BRIGADE
(PRINCE CONSORT'S OWN)

ORIGINATED AS the Experimental Rifle Corps in 1800. Badge: A Maltese cross inscribed with the regimental battle honours and surrounded by a laurel wreath, in the centre, a bugle horn. Motto: (that of the Prince Consort) *Treu und Fest.* Part of the Corps are the 15th City of London Regiment (London Rifle Brigade), and the 17th London Regiment (Tower Hamlet Rifles).

GRENADIER GUARDS

ONE OF the five regiments of Foot Guards which, like the Household Cavalry, forms an escort for the King on ceremonial occasions. Originated 1656 as 1st Foot Guards. Badge : A fired grenade ; Motto : *Honi Soit qui mal y Pensc.*

COLDSTREAM GUARDS

FORMED IN 1650, is oldest Guards regiment in the Army. Named from the Berwickshire town of Coldstream, whence it marched to restore Charles II to the throne. Badge : Star of the Order of the Garter ; Mottoes : *Honi Soit qui mal y Pensc* and *Nulli Secundus.*

SCOTS GUARDS

FORMED IN Scotland after the Restoration (1660) as the Third Font Guards. Became the Scots Guards in 1877. Badge : The Star of the Order of the Thistle ; Motto : *Nemo me impune lacessit.* Colonel-in-Chief, H.M. The King ; Colonel : The Duke of Gloucester.

IRISH GUARDS

ESTABLISHED BY Queen Victoria in 1900 in honour of the Irish regiments which fought in the South African War. Badge : The Star of the Order of St. Patrick ; Motto : *Quis Separabit ?* Colonel-in-Chief : H.M. The King.

WELSH GUARDS

THE FIRST battalion was raised in 1915 by King George V with Welshmen of the other Guards regiments as a nucleus. Second battalion was authorised in April, 1939. Badge : A Leek ; Motto : *Cymru-am-Byth.*

THE ROYAL SCOTS
(The Royal Regiment)

AFTER SERVICE in 1687 in Sweden and France the regiment was known as the Dumbarton Regiment ; it gained the name of the Royal Regiment for service at Tangier. Badge : Star of the Order of the Thistle, with St. Andrew and Cross in centre. Motto : *Nemo me impune lacessit.*

THE QUEEN'S ROYAL REGIMENT
(West Surrey)

FORMED IN 1661 by the Earl of Peterborough, the 22nd and 24th London Regiments (The Queen's) are part of the corps of this regiment. Badge : The Paschal Lamb (crest of the wife of Charles II, Catherine of Braganza, after whom the regiment was named) with Banner of St. George.

THE BUFFS
(The Royal East Kent Regiment)

RAISED IN 1572 by the citizens of London to serve in Holland. Its name " The Buffs " arose because at one time the regiment wore buff-coloured jackets. Badge : Dragon of the House of Tudor ; Motto : *Invicta.*

THE KING'S OWN
ROYAL REGIMENT
(Lancaster)

THE KING'S OWN was formed in 1680; has had several titles, the present coming in after the 1914-18 war. Served also as a marine regiment. Badge: The Lion of England; Motto: *Honi Soit qui mal y Pense.*

THE ROYAL
NORTHUMBERLAND FUSILIERS

FORMED IN 1674 in Flanders largely from Irishmen. It became the Northumberland Fusiliers in 1881. *Royal* added for services in the 1914-18 war. Badge: Fired grenade with St. George and the Dragon in the centre. Motto: *Quo Fata Vocant.*

THE
ROYAL WARWICKSHIRE
REGIMENT

THE WARWICKSHIRES, as the 6th Foot, were placed on the English establishment in 1688, after fighting for several years in Holland. Badge: An antelope, in memory of the regiment's victory at Saragossa (1710) when it captured a Moorish flag bearing the device of an antelope.

THE ROYAL FUSILIERS
(City of London Regiment)

RAISED BY James II, especially as fusiliers, it was formed from the old train bands of London, the fore-runners of the Territorials. In 1938 the 1st battalion became a machine-gun unit. Badge: A fired grenade; in the garter, a rose. Motto: *Honi Soit qui mal y Pense.*

THE KING'S REGIMENT
(Liverpool)

FORMED IN 1685 by James II as "Princess Anne of Denmark's Regiment." It became the King's Regiment in 1715, and the King's (Liverpool) Regiment in 1881.
Badge: The White Horse of Hanover in a prancing position.
Mottoes: *Nec aspera terrent* and *Honi Soit qui mal y Pense.*

THE ROYAL
NORFOLK REGIMENT

THE REGIMENT was raised in 1695.
Badge: Britannia; awarded after the battle of Almanza, in 1707, when it covered the retreat of the army.
Motto: *Honi Soit qui mal y Pense.*

THE LINCOLNSHIRE
REGIMENT

ESTABLISHED IN 1685. Badge: A Sphinx, won when fighting in Egypt in 1801. Motto: *Honi Soit qui mal y Pense.*

THE DEVONSHIRE
REGIMENT

FORMED IN 1685 with the name of the "Duke of Beaufort's Musketeers" and assumed its present title in 1881. Badge: Exeter Castle and the Crown. Motto: *Semper Fidelis.*

THE SUFFOLK REGIMENT

FORMED IN 1661 from the garrison of Windsor Castle, becoming the 12th (East Suffolk) Regiment of Foot in 1782. Badge: Gibraltar Castle, commemorating the siege; Motto: *Montes Insignia Calpe.*

THE SOMERSET LIGHT INFANTRY
(Prince Albert's)

FORMED IN 1685; known at one time as the 13th (Somersetshire) Prince Albert's Light Infantry. Badge: Bugle horn and mural crown; Motto: *Jellalabad*, an Indian City defended by the regiment.

THE WEST YORKSHIRE REGIMENT
(The Prince of Wales's Own)

ESTABLISHED IN 1685 as the 14th Foot, this regiment took its Yorkshire title in 1881. Badge: The White Horse of Hanover, granted by George III. Mottoes: *Nec Aspera terrent* and *Ich Dien.*

THE EAST YORKSHIRE REGIMENT
(The Duke of York's Own)

ESTABLISHED IN 1685 and received the second part of its title after the 1914-18 war. Badge: The Rose of York and laurel wreath; Motto: *Honi Soit qui mal y Pense.*

THE BEDFORDSHIRE & HERTFORDSHIRE REGIMENT

RAISED IN 1688, it has been, at different times, the Buckinghamshire and Leicestershire Regiment, and the 16th (Bedfordshire) Regiment, and in 1919 obtained its present designation. Badge: A buck crossing a ford; Motto: *Honi Soit qui mal y Pense.*

THE LEICESTERSHIRE REGIMENT

THE FIRST regiment of several to be raised by William III in the seventeenth century; one of the two still existing. Badge: A tiger, awarded for service in India and Afghanistan. Motto: *Honi Soit qui mal y Pense.*

THE GREEN HOWARDS
(Alexandra, Princess of Wales's Own Yorkshire Regiment)

FORMED IN 1688, becoming Alexandra, Princess of Wales's Own Yorkshire Regiment in 1901. In 1919 adopted an additional name after a commander, Howard who introduced green facings for the uniforms. Badge: The Danish Cross and the letter "A."

THE LANCASHIRE FUSILIERS

ESTABLISHED IN 1688, the only Fusilier Regiment not "Royal." Badge: A fired grenade, and a sphinx for service in Egypt surrounded by a laurel wreath, awarded to commemorate the battle of Minden (1759). Motto: *Omnia Audax.*

THE
ROYAL SCOTS FUSILIERS

THE OLDEST Fusilier Regiment and the second oldest Scottish regiment in the army. In 1938 the 1st battalion became a machine-gun unit. Badge: A fired grenade with the Royal Arms; Motto: *Nemo me impune lacessit.*

THE CHESHIRE REGIMENT

FORMED BY the Duke of Norfolk in 1689. Badge: Star with acorn and leaves, said to have been given to the regiment by George II. Motto: *Ich Dien.*

THE
ROYAL WELCH FUSILIERS

RAISED BY the 9th Lord Herbert of Cherbury in 1689 as Herbert's Regiment. Badge: Fired grenade with Prince of Wales's Feathers in the centre. Mottoes: *Ich Dien* and *Nec Aspera terrent.*

THE SOUTH WALES
BORDERERS

FORMED IN 1689, it became known in 1702 as "Churchill's Regiment" after the future Duke of Marlborough. Present title, 1881. Badge: The Sphinx, for service in Egypt, surrounded by a wreath of everlasting flowers.

THE KING'S OWN SCOTTISH BORDERERS

FOUNDED IN 1688. Badge: The Castle of Edinburgh and St. Andrew's Cross, surmounted by the Royal Crest. Mottoes: *Nisi Dominus Frustra* and *In Veritate Religionis Confido*. Colonel: H.R.H. The Duchess of Gloucester.

THE CAMERONIANS (Scottish Rifles)

FOUNDED IN 1689 from the Cameronians, who were Puritans, to support William of Orange. Every Presbyterian recruit of the 1st Battalion is presented with a Bible. Badge: A bugle horn and a star from the coat of arms of the Earl of Arran, first colonel of the regiment and a thistle wreath. Motto: *Nemo me impune lacessit.*

THE ROYAL INNISKILLING FUSILIERS

RAISED IN 1689. Between 1922 and 1937 it formed one corps with the Royal Irish Fusiliers (Princess Victoria's), but was separated again in 1937. Badge: Inniskilling Castle on a hand grenade. Colonel-in-Chief: H.R.H. The Duke of Gloucester. Motto: *Nec aspera terrent.*

THE GLOUCESTERSHIRE REGIMENT

FIRST BATTALION was raised in 1694. Wears two badges on its caps, one at the front and a similar smaller one at the back. The custom commemorates a back-to-back stand during the Battle of Alexandria, Egypt, 1801. Badge: A Sphinx encircled by a Laurel Wreath. Motto: *Honi Soit que mal y Pense.*

THE WORCESTERSHIRE REGIMENT

FIRST BATTALION was formed in 1694. Badge : The Star of the Order of the Garter with the Lion of the Royal Crest upon a pedestal inscribed with the Motto : Firm.

THE EAST LANCASHIRE REGIMENT

THE FIRST battalion was raised as a marine regiment in 1702, and became the 30th (Cambridgeshire) Regiment in 1782. It amalgamated with another regiment in 1881. Badge : The Rose of Lancaster with the Sphinx for service in Egypt. Motto : *Spectamur Agendo.*

THE EAST SURREY REGIMENT

RAISED AS a marine regiment in 1702 under the title of " Villiers Marines," the 1st battalion amalgamated with the Surrey regiment in 1881. Badge : A castle with a shield bearing the arms of Kingston-on-Thames on the central tower ; Motto : *Honi Soit qui mal y Pense.*

THE DUKE OF CORNWALLS LIGHT INFANTRY.

THE FIRST battalion was raised as a marine regiment in 1702 and took part in the capture of Gibraltar. Badge : Bugle horn and coronet of The Duke of Cornwall ; Motto : One and All.

THE DUKE OF WELLINGTON'S REGIMENT
(West Riding)

THE FIRST battalion was raised in 1702 and the Duke of Wellington was at one time its Commander. Badge : The Crest of the Duke of Wellington. Motto : *Virtutis Fortuna Comes.*

THE BORDER REGIMENT

FIRST BATTALION was formed in 1702 and the second in 1775. Badge : A Maltese Cross inscribed with the regiment's chief battle honours and encircled by a laurel wreath in memory of Fontenoy (1745). Motto: *Honi Soit qui mal y Pense.*

THE ROYAL SUSSEX REGIMENT

FIRST BATTALION was formed in 1702 as " Ponsonby's Regiment." It was the first British regiment to march right across India. Badge : The Star of the Order of the Garter with Roussillon Plume. Motto : *Honi Soit qui mal y Pense.*

THE MONMOUTHSHIRE REGIMENT

FORMED IN 1860 as the Monmouthshire Rifle Volunteer Corps. Part of the corps of the South Wales Borderers. First Battalion is a searchlight unit. Has a long list of battle honours. Badge : The Welsh Dragon.

THE SOUTH STAFFORDSHIRE REGIMENT

THE FIRST battalion was formed in 1702. Badge : The Stafford Knot, one of the old heraldic devices of the Lords of Stafford ; Motto : *Honi Soit qui mal y Pense.*

THE DORSETSHIRE REGIMENT

THE FIRST and second battalions were formed in 1702 and 1755 respectively, as marines. Regimental Badge : The Castle of Gibraltar, the Sphinx and the word " Marabout," in honour of service in Egypt. Mottoes : *Montis Insignia Calpe* and *Primus in Indis.*

THE PRINCE OF WALES'S VOLUNTEERS
(South Lancashire)

BADGE AND title were given first to the regiment that is now the 2nd Battalion by George IV as Prince of Wales. Badge : Prince of Wales's Feathers with the Sphinx for service in Egypt ; Motto : *Ich Dien.* The ranks are called " Volunteers " and not " Privates."

THE WELCH REGIMENT

ORIGINATED AS the 1st Invalids Regiment, formed from out-pensioners of the Royal Hospital, Chelsea, in 1719. In 1822 it became the 41st (The Welch) Regiment of Foot. Badge : The Prince of Wales's Feathers ; Motto : *Ich Dien.*

THE BLACK WATCH
(Royal Highlanders)

THE SENIOR Highland regiment. Badge : The Star of the Order of the Thistle with St. Andrew in the centre holding his cross ; Motto : *Nemo me impune Lacessit.* Colonel-in-Chief : H.M. The Queen.

THE OXFORDSHIRE AND BUCKINGHAMSHIRE LIGHT INFANTRY

THE 1st and 2nd battalions were formed in 1741 and 1755 respectively. Badge : A bugle horn ; Motto : *Honi Soit qui mal y Pense.*

THE ESSEX REGIMENT

FORMED IN 1881 from the 44th Foot, or East Essex Regiment, and the 56th Foot. Badge : The sphinx and the Castle of Gibraltar ; Motto : *Montis Insignia Calpe.*

THE SHERWOOD FORESTERS
(Nottinghamshire and Derbyshire Regiment)

THE FIRST battalion was raised as marines in 1740 and the second battalion in 1827. Badge : A Maltese Cross with the figure of a stag in the centre surrounded by a wreath of oak leaves. Motto : *Honi Soit qui mal y Pense.*

THE LOYAL REGIMENT
(North Lancashire)

THE REGIMENT was formed in 1881 from the 47th (Lancashire) Regiment and the Loyal Lincoln Volunteers. Badge : Rose of Lancaster with the Royal Crest ; Motto : *Loyauté M'Oblige.*

THE NORTHAMPTONSHIRE REGIMENT

FIRST BATTALION was formed in 1740 as the 48th (Northamptonshire) Regiment and the second battalion in 1755 as the 58th (Rutlandshire) Regiment. They combined in 1881. Badge : The Castle of Gibraltar ; Motto : *Montis Insignia Calpe.* Colonel-in-Chief : H.R.H. The Duchess of Gloucester.

THE ROYAL BERKSHIRE REGIMENT
(Princess Charlotte of Wales's)

FORMED FROM the merging of the Hertfordshire (Princess of Wales's) Regiment and the 66th Foot in 1881. Badge : The Chinese Dragon given for service in China. Motto : *Honi Soit qui mal y Pense.*

THE QUEEN'S OWN ROYAL WEST KENT REGIMENT

THE FIRST battalion was formed in 1756 and the second in 1824. Eighteen battalions served in the last war. The 20th London Regiment (Queen's Own) is part of the Corps of the Queen's Royal West Kent. Badge : The White Horse of Kent ; Motto : *Invicta.*

THE KING'S OWN YORKSHIRE LIGHT INFANTRY

FORMED IN 1881 from the 51st King's Own Light Infantry (2nd Yorkshire West Riding) Regiment and the 105th Foot. Badge: A French hunting horn and a rose. Motto; *Cede Nullis.* Colonel-in-Chief: H.M. The Queen.

THE KING'S SHROPSHIRE LIGHT INFANTRY

ITS FIRST battalion was formed in 1755 and the second in 1793. Badge: A bugle horn. Motto: *Aucto Splendore Resurgo.*

THE MIDDLESEX REGIMENT
(Duke of Cambridge's Own)

THE REGIMENT was formed in 1881 with the merging of the 57th (West Middlesex) regiment and the 77th (East Middlesex) regiment. Badge: The Prince of Wales's Plume and the coronet and cipher of the late Duke of Cambridge. Motto: *Ich Dien.*

THE KING'S ROYAL RIFLE CORPS

FIRST RIFLE Regiment in the Army with the longest list of honours. Formed in North America in 1755. Badge: The Maltese Cross with the Crown. Motto: *Celer et Audax,* conferred by General Wolfe.

THE
WILTSHIRE REGIMENT
(Duke of Edinburgh's)

THE FIRST battalion was raised in 1756 and the second in 1827. Badge : A cross with the coronet and cipher of the late Duke of Edinburgh in the centre. Motto : *Honi Soit qui mal y Pense.*

THE
MANCHESTER REGIMENT

IT WAS formed in 1881 from the West Suffolk Regiment and the 96th Foot. Badge : The Fleur-de-lys, first worn in 1930, replacing the arms of the City of Manchester ; Motto : *Honi Soit qui mal y Pense.*

THE
NORTH STAFFORDSHIRE
REGIMENT
(The Prince of Wales's)

ESTABLISHED IN 1881 from the 64th Foot and the 98th Foot. The history of the former regiment dates back to 1756. Badge : The Stafford Knot and the Prince of Wales' Feathers. Motto : *Ich Dien.*

THE
YORK AND LANCASTER
REGIMENT

THE FIRST battalion was raised in 1756 and the second in 1758. Badge : The tiger, denoting service in India and the union rose, the symbol of both York and Lancaster. Motto : *Honi Soit qui mal y Pense.*

THE GORDON HIGHLANDERS

FIRST BATTALION was formed in 1787 by the Duke of Gordon, and the second in 1797 by his son, the Marquis of Huntley. The 75th Foot and the 92nd Foot, as the battalions were then known, merged in 1881. Badge : The stag's head, the crest of the Gordon family, and the ivy wreath, the badge of the Gordon clan. Motto : *Bydand*. The 14th London Regiment (London Scottish) is part of the Corps.

THE HIGHLAND LIGHT INFANTRY
(City of Glasgow Regiment)

FORMED ON the merging in 1881 of the 71st Foot and 74th Foot. Badge : The Star of the Order of the the Thistle with a hunting horn in the centre and the initials H.L.I. The elephant at the base is in memory of the battle of Assaye, India, 1803. The regiment wears the Mackenzie tartan. Motto : *Montis Insignia Calpe*.

THE CAMBRIDGESHIRE REGIMENT

FORMED IN 1860 as the Cambridge Battalion of the Suffolk Regiment. Badge : The Castle of Cambridge and a shield bearing the arms of Ely.

THE DURHAM LIGHT INFANTRY

FORMED IN 1881 by the amalgamation of the 68th Durham Light Infantry and the 106th Bombay Light Infantry. Badge : A hunting horn with the initials D.L.I. ; Motto : *Honi Soit qui mal y Pense*.

THE QUEEN'S OWN CAMERON HIGHLANDERS

FORMED FROM the Cameron clan in 1793 by Sir Alan Cameron of Erracht. Awarded the title of Queen's Own in 1873. Badge : A wreath of thistles and St. Andrew holding his cross. Colonel-in-Chief : H.M. The King.

THE ROYAL ULSTER RIFLES

FORMED IN 1881 from the 83rd (County of Dublin) Regiment and the 86th (Royal County Down) Regiment. Badge : The Harp of Ireland and the crown. Motto : *Quis Separabit ?*

THE ROYAL IRISH FUSILIERS
(Princess Victoria's)

FORMED IN 1793. Badge : A flaming hand grenade with an eagle, commemorating the capture of the first French Eagle standard in the Peninsular War. Among its mottoes is *Faugh-a-Ballagh.*

THE ARGYLL AND SUTHERLAND HIGHLANDERS
(Princess Louise's)

TWO FAMOUS highland regiments which merged in 1881. Badge : A boar's head, the crest of the Campbells, Duke of Argyll, and a wild cat, ctres of the Sutherland family ; the coronet and cipher of Princess Louise within a thistle wreath. Mottoes : *Ne Obliviscaris* and *Sans Peur.*

ROYAL ARMY SERVICE CORPS

RESPONSIBLE FOR the supplies of the Army. Established in 1794 and earned the title of " Royal " for its services in the 1914-18 war. Badge : The Royal Cipher encircled with a laurel wreath ; Motto : *Honi Soit qui mal y Pense.*

ROYAL ARMY ORDNANCE CORPS

DEALS WITH the armament and equipment of the army. Its history goes back to 1418, and from the middle of the fifteenth century till the nineteenth, the Ordnance Department was at the Tower of London. In 1881 it became the Ordnance Store Corps. Badge : Arms of the Board of Ordnance. Motto : *Honi soit qui mal y Pense.*

ROYAL ARMY MEDICAL CORPS

THE R.A.M.C. was established in 1873 and the only two bars to the V.C. ever awarded were gained by members of the corps Badge : The rod of Æsculapius, ancient God of healing, a serpent and a laurel wreath ; Motto : *In Arduis Fidelis.*

ROYAL ARMY VETERINARY CORPS

CARES FOR the animals in the army; established in 1795. Badge : The Figure of Chiron, a legendary being, half man, half horse, but an expert healer. Services in the last war gained them the title " Royal."

LOVAT'S SCOUTS

THE SCOTTISH
HORSE SCOUTS

9th BATTALION
HIGHLAND
LIGHT INFANTRY

THE HERTFORDSHIRE
REGIMENT

THE HEREFORDSHIRE
REGIMENT

1st BATTALION
THE MONMOUTHSHIRE
REGIMENT

5th CITY OF LONDON REGIMENT
(London Rifle Brigade)

HEADS THE City of London Regiments. Founded in 1859 when the Volunteers became official. Badge: The arms of the Royal Standard surrounded by a wreath inscribed with battle honours gained in South Africa, France and Flanders. Motto: *Primus in Urbe.*

6th CITY OF LONDON REGIMENT
(City of London Rifles)

DATES BACK to 1861. Now an anti-aircraft battalion. Badge: A Maltese Cross, with a stringed bugle in the centre. Motto: *Domine Dirige Nos.*

7th CITY OF LONDON REGIMENT.
(Post Office Rifles)

G.P.O. WORKERS were used as special constables in 1867 to deal with Irish terrorism. From them a volunteer regiment was formed. Now an anti-aircraft unit. Badge: A flaming hand grenade with number 7.

9th LONDON REGIMENT
(Queen Victoria's Rifles)

FORMED IN 1908 from the Victoria and St. George's Rifles. Claims to be the second oldest unit of the Territorial Army. The St. George's Rifles were formed in 1792 on the initiative of householders of Hanover Square. The Victoria Rifles descend from the Covent Garden Volunteers formed in 1798. Badge: The Maltese Cross with St. George and the Dragon in the centre. Motto: *Vis Unita Fortior.*

10th LONDON REGIMENT
(Hackney)

FOUGHT IN the 1914-18 war in France, Gallipoli, Egypt and Palestine. Badge : The Hackney Tower in centre : Motto : *Justitia Turris Nostra.*

11th LONDON REGIMENT
(Finsbury Rifles)

DESCENDANTS OF the Loyal Clerkenwell Association raised in 1797 and disbanded in 1814, and of the Clerkenwell Rifle Volunteer Corps, formed in 1859. Now an anti-aircraft brigade.

12th LONDON REGIMENT
(Rangers)

ONE OF the Volunteer (pre-Territorial Army) units formed in 1859, but descended from the "Gentlemen Members of Grays Inn," a force formed in 1780. Badge : The Maltese Cross with the bugle horn in the centre. Motto is "Exel." Other ranks are known as "riflemen" and not "privates."

13th LONDON REGIMENT
(Princess Louise's Kensington Regiment)

FORMED AS a result of the Volunteer (pre-Territorial Army) movement of 1859 by Lord Truro. Headquarters moved from Islington to West London and its present title taken in 1913. Adopted the Arms of the Royal Borough of Kensington as its badge in 1905 with its motto of *Quid Nobis Ardui.*

THE 14th
LONDON REGIMENT
(The London Scottish)

SENT THE first Territorial battalion to France in the last war. Formed in 1859 amongst other Volunteer (pre-Territorial Army) units by Scottish citizens of London. Badge: The Lion of Scotland over a St. Andrew Cross, surrounded by a border of thistles. Motto: *Strike Sure.*

16th LONDON REGIMENT
(Queen's Westminster
and Civil Service Rifles)

DESCENDS FROM the Pimlico Regiment of 1793, and amalgamated with other Westminster Companies in 1860. The Civil Service Rifles was formed in 1859 from members of the Audit and Post Office departments, Inland Revenue, British Museum, Courts of Justice, Bank of England and others. Merged with the Queen's Westminsters in 1921.

17th LONDON REGIMENT
(Tower Hamlets Rifles)

RE-FORMED IN 1859 amongst other Volunteer regiments. Originally numbered amongst its ranks many men from a famous brewery firm.

18th LONDON REGIMENT
(London Irish Rifles)

FORMED IN 1859 sponsored by well-known Irishmen in London. Lord Palmerston joined as a private. Badge: The Irish harp surrounded by a wreath of shamrock leaves.

19th LONDON REGIMENT
(St. Pancras)

A St. Pancras Volunteer Corps existed as far back as 1798—and probably earlier. The regiment was formed in 1859. Now an anti-aircraft battalion. Badge: The Maltese Cross surrounded by a laurel wreath.

20th LONDON REGIMENT
(The Queen's Own)

Dates back to 1859 and recruited many men from Woolwich Arsenal. Is part of the Corps of the Queen's Own Royal West Kent Regiment. Now an anti-aircraft unit. Motto: *Invicta.*

21st LONDON REGIMENT
(First Surrey Rifles)

Dates back to 1798, when it was known as the 1st Regiment of Surrey Volunteers. Now an anti-aircraft battalion. Badge: A Maltese Cross with a bugle horn in the centre. Motto: *Concordia Victrix.*

23rd LONDON REGIMENT
(The East Surrey Regiment)

Descendants of the Newington (Surrey) Volunteers of 1789, disbanded in 1815. Revived in 1859 with the beginning of the Volunteer movement. Motto: *Loyalty Unites Us.* Badge: A Castle on an eight-pointed star.

28th LONDON REGIMENT
(Artists Rifles)

**THE INNS OF COURT
REGIMENT**

**THE ROYAL SUSSEX
REGIMENT**
(5th Battalion Cinque Ports)

THE BUCKS BATTALION
(Oxfordshire and
Buckinghamshire
Light Infantry)

**KING'S OWN MALTA
REGIMENT**

**ROYAL
GUERNSEY MILITIA**

**7th BATTALION THE
SHERWOOD FORESTERS**
(The Robin Hoods)

**THE
HAMPSHIRE REGIMENT**

**THE SOUTH WALES
BORDERERS**
(Brecknockshire Battalion)

**THE HAMPSHIRE
REGIMENT**
6th (Duke of Connaught's
Own) Battalion

**7th BATTALION
THE HAMPSHIRE
REGIMENT**

**8th BATTALION
THE HAMPSHIRE
REGIMENT**
(The Princess Beatrice's
Isle of Wight Rifles)

THE WEST YORKSHIRE
REGIMENT
(7th/8th Battalion
Prince of Wales's Own)

THE
SEAFORTH HIGHLANDERS
(5th Battalion) (T.A.)

THE WARWICKSHIRE
YEOMANRY

THE YORKSHIRE HUSSARS
(Alexandra,
Princess of Wales's Own)

THE STAFFORDSHIRE
YEOMANRY
(Queen's Own Royal
Regiment)

THE NOTTINGHAMSHIRE
YEOMANRY
(Sherwood Rangers)

THE SHROPSHIRE
YEOMANRY

THE AYRSHIRE
YEOMANRY
(Earl of Garrick's Own)

THE CHESHIRE
YEOMANRY
(Earl of Chester's)

THE
YORKSHIRE DRAGOONS
(Queen's Own)

THE LEICESTERSHIRE
YEOMANRY
(Prince Albert's Own)

THE NORTH SOMERSET
YEOMANRY

THE DUKE OF
LANCASTER'S OWN
YEOMANRY

THE LANARKSHIRE
YEOMANRY

THE NORTHUMBERLAND
HUSSARS

DUKE OF YORK'S
OWN LOYAL
SUFFOLK HUSSARS

THE HAMPSHIRE
YEOMANRY

QUEEN'S OWN
DORSET YEOMANRY

THE QUEEN'S
OWN WORCESTERSHIRE
HUSSARS

THE ROYAL DEVON
YEOMANRY

THE BEDFORDSHIRE
YEOMANRY

THE ESSEX
YEOMANRY

THE GLAMORGAN
YEOMANRY

THE NORFOLK
YEOMANRY
(The King's Own
Royal Regiment)

THE
SOUTH
NOTTINGHAMSHIRE
HUSSARS

QUEEN'S OWN
OXFORDSHIRE HUSSARS

THE
NORTHAMPTONSHIRE
YEOMANRY

THE LOTHIAN
AND BORDER
YEOMANRY

THE ROYAL
GLOUCESTERSHIRE
HUSSARS

1st LONDON YEOMANRY
(Middlesex, Duke of Cambridge's
Hussars)

ROYAL ARMY PAY CORPS

THE ARMY DENTAL CORPS

ARMY EDUCATIONAL
CORPS

AUXILIARY
MILITARY PIONEER CORPS

ROYAL
MILITARY COLLEGE
SANDHURST

THE GENERAL LIST

OFFICER'S
FORAGE
CAP
BADGE
R.A.F.

ROYAL AIR FORCE
(Cap Badge)

ROYAL AIR FORCE
(Cap Badge)

CAP BADGE worn by officers below air rank consists of the Crown, Eagle and Wreath. Officers of the W.A.A.F. and the Princess Mary's R.A.F. Nursing Service wear a similar badge. Rankers and members of the Women's Auxiliary Air Force wear the monogram R.A.F., surrounded by a wreath and surmounted by a crown.

ROYAL AIR FORCE
(Pilot's Wings)

ROYAL AIR FORCE
MEDICAL SERVICE
COLLAR BADGE

OBSERVER

GUNNER

EMBLEMS OF AIR FORCE RANKS

MARSHAL OF THE ROYAL AIR FORCE

AIR CHIEF MARSHAL

AIR MARSHAL

AIR VICE-MARSHAL

AIR COMMODORE

GROUP CAPTAIN

WING COMMANDER

SQUADRON LEADER

FLIGHT-LIEUTENANT

FLYING OFFICER

PILOT OFFICER

INDIAN EMPIRE

5th KING EDWARD'S OWN PROBYN'S HORSE

9th ROYAL DECCAN HORSE

10th QUEEN VICTORIA'S OWN CORPS OF GUIDES (Cavalry Frontier Force)

11th PRINCE ALBERT VICTOR'S OWN (Cavalry Frontier Force)

14th PRINCE OF WALES' OWN SCINDE HORSE

1st KING GEORGE'S OWN GURKHA RIFLES (The Malaun Regiment)

20th BURMA RIFLES

1st MADRAS PIONEERS

1st PUNJAB REGIMENT

15th PUNJAB REGIMENT

8th PUNJAB REGIMENT

3rd CAVALRY

THE DOMINIONS
AUSTRALIA

AUSTRALIAN
COMMONWEALTH
MILITARY FORCES
(General Service Badge)

THE CAP badge of the Australian Imperial Force does not represent the sun as is popularly supposed. It originated as a badge for a regiment of light horse that was the first Federal contingent to serve in the South African War, and was designed to imitate a trophy of arms—swords and bayonets surrounding an imperial crown. Designers, however, varied the pattern until the original design is almost lost. The Royal Australian Navy and the Royal Australian Air Force are powerful units of defence.

CANADA

CANADIAN REGIMENTAL badges are distinguished by their individuality and variety of design. 628,462 Canadians served in the 1914–18 war. Made history at Ypres in 1915, where poison gas was first used. To-day there is a constant stream of Canadian soldiers and airmen to the fronts. Has its own Air Force and Navy.

NEW ZEALAND

NEW ZEALANDERS are now serving in the Near and Middle East. They fought for Britain in the Boer War of 1899-1902. In the 1914–18 war 128,525 joined the colours. Has its own Navy and Air Force.

SOUTH AFRICA

IN THE 1914–18 war 221,500 South Africans served in the different theatres of war, mainly in West, Central and South-West Africa. Generals were Botha, Smuts and Van Deventer. Fought also in France. Has its own Air Force.

The INDIAN EMPIRE

THE INDIAN Army is composed of both British and Indian soldiers. The Native States have their own armies which are at the service of the Empire. In 1934, the Royal Indian Marine Service became the Royal Indian Navy. There is also an Indian Air Force.

CANADA

ROYAL CANADIAN
CORPS OF SIGNALS

LORD STRATHCONA'S
HORSE,
ROYAL CANADIANS

THE EDMONTON
REGIMENT

ROYAL CANADIAN
ORDNANCE CORPS

ROYAL CANADIAN
DRAGOONS

THE LINCOLN
REGIMENT

THE WEYBURN
REGIMENT

FORT GARRY HORSE

10th BRANT DRAGOONS

19th ALBERTA
DRAGOONS

CANADIAN GENERAL
SERVICE BADGE

ROYAL CANADIAN
ARMY MEDICAL CORPS

CANADA

QUEEN'S RANGERS
(1st Americans)

THE WENTWORTH
REGIMENT

THE ELGIN
REGIMENT

ROYAL CANADIAN
ARMY SERVICE CORPS

EDMONTON
FUSILIERS

2nd DRAGOONS

LE REGIMENT
DE MAISONNEUVE

CANADIAN SCOTTISH

ROYAL MONTREAL
REGIMENT

INFANTERIE
DE JOLIETTE

CANADIAN
MACHINE GUN
CORPS

ASSINIBOIA
REGIMENT

CANADA

PRINCESS LOUISE
DRAGOON GUARDS

ROYAL CANADIAN
ENGINEERS

11th CANADIAN
REGIMENT

3rd PRINCE OF WALES
CANADIAN DRAGOONS

12th MANITOBA
DRAGOONS

3rd TORONTO
REGIMENT

CANADIAN ARMY
VETERINARY CORPS

PRINCESS PATRICIA'S
CANADIAN LIGHT
INFANTRY

HIGHLAND
LIGHT INFANTRY
OF CANADA

THE YORKTON
REGIMENT

LE REGIMENT
DE HULL

THE
ROYAL HIGHLANDERS
OF CANADA

SOUTH AFRICA

**S.A. MACHINE GUN
SQUADRON**

S.A CADETS

**PRETORIA
REGIMENT**
(Princess Alice's Own)

**S.A. SPECIAL SERVICE
BATTALION**

**REGIMENT SOUTH
WESTERN DISTRICT**

**PRINCE ALFRED'S
GUARD**

**REGIMENT
WESTERN PROVINCE**

**DISTRICT
MOUNTED RIFLES**

**REGIMENT
LOUW WEPENER**

**TRANSVAAL
SCOTTISH REGIMENT**

REGIMENT BOTHA

**S.A. GENERAL
OFFICERS**

SOUTH AFRICA

S.A. VETERINARY
CORPS

RAND LIGHT
INFANTRY

NATAL DISTRICT
RIFLE ASSOCIATION

CAPE PENINSULAR
RIFLES

DURBAN LIGHT
INFANTRY

CAPE TOWN
HIGHLANDERS

KIMBERLEY
REGIMENT

WITWATERSRAND
RIFLES

S.A. SIGNALS CORPS

S.A. ARTILLERY
REGIMENT

S.A. AIR FORCE

S.A. PAY CORPS

SOUTH AFRICA

NATAL
MOUNTED RIFLES

UMVOTI
MOUNTED RIFLES

REGIMENT
PRESIDENT STEYN

S.A. MEDICAL CORPS

REGIMENT DE WET

REGIMENT DE LA REY

ROYAL NATAL
CARABINIERS

S.A. INSTRUCTIONAL
CORPS

S.A. ORDNANCE
CORPS

S.A. CORPS OF
MILITARY POLICE

S.A. ARMY SERVICE
CORPS

S.A. ENGINEERS
CORPS

CIVIL DEFENCE UNITS

THE NEEDS of civil defence have produced a number of new bodies based on established organisations such as the Police Force with its Special Constabulary and War Reserve. The Fire Brigades are supplemented by the Auxiliary Fire Service, which enrols both men and women. The Air Raid Precautions service is an entirely new growth. The first A.R.P. department of the Home Office was formed in 1935.

WOMEN'S and NURSING SERVICES

THREE WOMEN'S services are organised in conjunction with the armed forces. They are the Women's Royal Naval Service the Women's Auxiliary Territorial Service and the Women's Auxiliary Air Force. The two latter are of recent formation, the first dating back to the 1914–18 war. Members of all three services relieve men from many clerical, culinary, storekeeping and other specialist duties. Organisations such as the Women's Legion, the Women's Transport Service (F.A.N.Y.) and the Mechanised Transport Corps, work both at home and overseas. Their cars and drivers work for the civilian and nursing services. They have distinctive uniforms and badges. The Women's Land Army supplement farm labour where shortage occurs. Nursing services are represented by the Queen Alexandra's Imperial Military Nursing Service originated by Florence Nightingale, Queen Alexandra's Royal Navy Nursing Sisters, and Princess Mary's Royal Air Force Nursing Service. They are the " regulars." The British Red Cross Society and the Order of St. John of Jerusalem, the latter the oldest order of chivalry in the world, who have combined for the " duration," care for sick and wounded soldiers and civilians, prisoners of war and shipwrecked mariners. Many of their members nurse. The recently formed Civil Nursing Reserve supplements nursing staff where needed in hospitals, First Aid Posts or with the District Nurses in reception areas. Women's Voluntary Services do work of all kimds.

N.A.A.F.I. and E.N.S.A.

THE NAVY, Army and Air Force Institutes (N.A.A.F.I.) supplies the greater part of the Army's rations when at home and does much for their comfort in all directions when overseas. Attached to it is E.N.S.A., the Entertainment National Service Association, promoted by members of the entertainment profession.

CIVIL DEFENCE UNITS

METROPOLITAN
POLICE
(Inspectors)

METROPOLITAN
POLICE
(Cap Badge, Sergeants
and Constables)

METROPOLITAN
POLICE
(Helmet Badge,
height 4½ inches)

METROPOLITAN
SPECIAL
CONSTABULARY
(Commandant and
Assistant Commandant)

METROPOLITAN
SPECIAL
CONSTABULARY
(Inspectors and
Sub-Inspectors)

METROPOLITAN
SPECIAL
CONSTABULARY
(Sergeants and
Constables)

AUXILIARY
FIRE SERVICE

AIR RAID PRECAUTIONS

CIVIL NURSING
RESERVE

ENTERTAINMENTS
NATIONAL SERVICE
ASSOCIATION

WOMEN'S
VOLUNTEER SERVICE

WOMEN'S & NURSING SERVICES

NAVY ARMY & AIR FORCE
INSTITUTES

AUXILIARY
TERRITORIAL SERVICE

WOMEN'S LAND ARMY

THE WOMEN'S LEGION

WOMEN'S
TRANSPORT SERVICE

MECHANISED TRANSPORT
TRAINING CORPS

QUEEN ALEXANDRA'S
ROYAL NAVAL NURSING
SISTERS
(Hat Badge, Gold)

QUEEN
ALEXANDR A'S
IMPERIAL MILITARY
NURSING SERVICE

WAR ORGANISATION OF
BRITISH
RED CROSS SOCIETY &
ORDER OF ST. JOHN
(Headquarters Personnel)

BRITISH RED CROSS
SOCIETY

WAR ORGANISATION OF
BRITISH
RED CROSS SOCIETY &
ORDER OF ST JOHN
(For Personnel serving
Overseas)

ST JOHN AMBULANCE
BRIGADE

MOTTOES and their MEANINGS

Arma Pacis Fulcra = Peace Based on Arms.
Aucto Splendore Resurgo = I Rise with Increased Splendour.
Bon Coeur et Bon Bras = Strong Heart and Strong Arm.
Bydand = Watchful.
Cede Nullis = Yield to None.
Celer et Audax = Swift and Bold.
Cirta Cito = Fast and Sure.
Concordia Victrix = Unity is Victorious.
Cuidich'n Righ = Help to the King.
Cymru-Am-Byth = Wales for Ever.
Decus et Tutamen = Honour and Security.
Dieu et Mon Droit = God and my Right.
Domine Dirige Nos = Lord Direct Us.
Eendrag Maak Mag = Union is Strength.
Faugh-a-Ballagh = Clear the Way.
Fide et Fiducia = By Faith and Confidence.
Fidelis = Faithful.
Floreat Bloemfontein = Flourish Bloemfontein !
Honi Soit qui mal y Pense = Evil be to them who Evil think.
Ich Dien = I Serve.
Inter Arma Caritas = Humanity in War.
In Arduis Fidelis = Faithful in Difficulty.
In Veritate Religionis Confido = To Trust in the Truth of Religion.
Invicta = Unconquered.
Justitia Turris Nostra = Justice is our Tower.
Labor Omnia Vincit = Work Conquers all.
Loyauté M'Oblige = Loyalty Binds Me.
Mente et Manu = With Heart and Hand.
Merebimur = We will Observe.
Montes Insignia Calpe = The Badge of the Rock of Gibraltar.
Ne Obliviscaris = Do Not Let Us Forget.
Nec Aspera Terrent = Nor Do Difficulties Deter Us.
Nemo Me Impune Lacessit = No One May Touch Me with Impunity.
Nisi Dominus Frustra = Unless God be with Us all is Vain.
Non Nobis Sed Patriœ = Not Ourselves but our Country.
Nulli Secundus = Second to None.
Officium Primum = Duty First.
Omnia Audax = Bold in Everything.
On ne Passe Pas = They Shall Not Pass.
Ons Waarsku = Beware.
Ora et Labora = Pray and Work.
Per Mare Per Terram = By Land and Sea.
Primus in Africa = First in Africa.
Primus in Indis = First in India.
Primus in Urbe = First in the City.
Pristinœ Virtutis Memores = Mindful of former Valour.
Pro Aris et Focis = For Hearth and Home.
Pro Deo Rege Patria = For God, King and Country.
Progredere ne Regredere = Advance and Not Retreat.
Pro Patria = For Country.

Pro Regi et Imperio = For King and Empire.
Quem Timebo = Whom Shall I Fear ?
Quid Nobis Ardui = Nothing too Hard for Us.
Quis Separabit ? = Who Shall Separate Us ?
Quo Fas et Gloria Ducunt = Where Duty and Glory Lead.
Quo Fata Vocant = Wherever the Fates May Call.
Sans Peur = Without Fear.
Semper Fidelis = Always Faithful.
Spectamur Agendo = Let Us be Judged by our Actions.
Thaba Bosigo = Black Mountain.
Treu und Fest = Loyal and Steadfast.
Tutela Bellicæ Virtutis = The Warrior's Defence is Courage.
Ubique = Everywhere.
Velox Versutus Vigilans = Swift, Skilful, Watchful.
Vestigia Nulla Retrorsum = We Never Retire.
Vires Acquirit Eundo = Acquire Strength by Progress.
Virtutis Fortuna Comes = Fortune Favours the Brave.
Vis Unita Fortior = Unity Increases Strength.
Voorwarts = Forward.

INDEX

Air Arm, Fleet (Pilot's Wings) 5
„ Force, Royal, Badges 47
„ „ „ Emblems of Rank 48
„ „ S.A. 55
„ Raid Precautions 58
Alberta Dragoons (19th) 51
Alexandra, Pss. of Wales's Own (York Hrs.) 41
„ „ „ „ York R. ... 21
Alexandra's, Queen, Imp. Mil. Nursing Service 59
„ „ R.N. Nursing Sisters ... 59
Americans, 1st (Queen's Rangers) 52
Argyll and Sutherland Highlanders 32
Army, British, Badge of 4
„ Emblems of Rank 7
Artillery Company, Honourable 14
„ Malta, Royal 14
„ Royal Regiment of 14
„ S.A. Regiment 55
Artists' Rifles (28th Lond. R.) 39
Assiniboia Regiment 52
Australian Commonwealth (General Service) ... 50
Auxiliary Fire Service 58
„ Military Pioneer Corps 46
„ Territorial Service 59
Ayrshire Yeomanry (Earl of Garrick's Own) ... 42

Bedfordshire & Hertfordshire Regiment ... 21
„ Yeomanry 44
Berkshire Regiment, The Royal 28
Black Watch, Royal Highlanders 27
Border, Yeomanry, Lothian and 45
„ Regiment 25
Borderers, King's Own Scottish 23
„ South Wales 22
Botha Regiment 54
Brant Dragoons (10th) 51
British Army, Badge of 15
„ Red Cross Society, The 59

Buckinghamshire Bn. (The Oxf. and Bucks. L.I.) 39
„ Oxf. and Lt. Inf. 27
Buffs (The Royal East Kent Regiment) 17
Burma Rifles (20th) 49

Cadets, S.A. 54
Canada, Royal Highlanders of 53
Canadian Army Medical Corps, Royal 51
„ „ Service Corps, Royal ... 52
„ „ Veterinary Corps ... 53
„ Corps of Signals 51
„ Dragoons, 2nd 52
„ Dragoons (3rd P. of Wales) ... 53
„ „ Royal 51
„ Engineers, Royal 51
„ General, Service Badge 51
„ Light Infantry (Pss. Patricia's) ... 53
„ Lord Strathcona's Horse, Royal ... 51
„ Machine Gun Corps 52
„ Ordnance Corps, Royal 51
„ Regiment, 11th 53
„ Scottish 52

Cambridgeshire Regiment 31
Cameron Highlanders 32
Cameronians (Scottish Rifles) 23
Cape Peninsula Rifles 55
„ Town Highlanders 55
Carabiniers, 3rd 9
„ (Royal Natal) 56
Cavalry Frontier Force 49
Cheshire Regiment 22
„ Yeomanry 42
Cinque Ports Bn. (R. Sussex R.) 39
Civil Nursing Reserve 58
„ Service Rifles 37
Coldstream Guards 16

Cavalry (3rd), India 49
Cavalry, Frontier Force 49

Deccan Horse (9th), Royal 49
De La Rey Regiment 56
Dental Corps, The Army 46
Derbyshire, Notts. and, Regiment 27
Devon Yeomanry, Royal 44
Devonshire Regiment 19
De Wet Regiment 56
District Mounted Rifles 54
Dorset Yeomanry 43
Dorsetshire Regiment 26
Dragoon Guards 1st (King's) 8
  „   „   2nd (The Queen's Bays) ... 8
  „   „   3rd (Prince of Wales's) ... 9
  „   „   4th/7th (Royal) 9
  „   „   5th Royal Inniskilling ... 9
  „   „   (Princess Louise) ... 53
Dragoons, 1st (The Royal) 9
  „   2nd (The Royal Scots Greys) ... 10
  „   2nd (Canadians) 52
Duke of Albany's (Seaforth Highlanders) ... 13
  „   Cambridge's Own 29
  „   Connaught's Own Bn. 40
  „   Cornwall's Light Infantry 24
  „   Edinburgh's (Wilts. R) 30
  „   Lancaster's Own Yeomanry 43
  „   Wellington's Regiment (West Riding)... 25
  „   York's Own Loyal Suffolk Hussars ... 43
Durban Light Infantry 55
Durham Light Infantry 31

Earl of Chester's (Ches. Yeomanry) 42
  „   Garrick's Own (Ayr. Yeomanry) ... 42
East Kent Regiment, Royal (The Buffs)... ... 17
  „   Lancashire Regiment 24
  „   Surrey Regiment 24
  „   „   (23rd Lond. R.) ... 38
  „   Yorkshire Regiment 20
Edmonton Fusiliers 52
  „   Regiment, The 51
Educational Corps, Army 46
Elgin Regiment, The 52
Engineers, Canadian, Royal 53
  „   Corps of, Royal 14
  „   Corps, S.A. 56
Entertainments National Service Association ... 58
Essex Regiment 27
  „   Yeomanry 44

Finsbury Rifles (11th Lond. R.) 36
Fire Service, Auxiliary 58
Fleet Air Arm (Pilot's Wings) 5
Foresters, Sherwood 27
Fort Garry Horse 51
Fusiliers, Edmonton 52
  „   Inniskilling, Royal 23
  „   Irish, Royal 32
  „   Lancashire 21
  „   Northumberland 18
  „   Royal 18
  „   Scots, Royal 22
  „   Welch, Royal 22

Garry Horse, Fort 51
General List, The 46

General Officers, S.A. 54
Glamorgan Yeomanry 44
Glasgow Regiment, City of (H.L.I.) 31
Gloucestershire Hussars Royal 45
  „   Regiment 23
Gordon Highlanders 31
Green Howards 21
Grenadier Guards 16
Guard, Prince Alfred's 54
Guards, Dragoon (1st King's) 8
  „   Life 8
  „   Royal Horse 8
Guernsey Militia, Royal 39
Guides, Queen Victoria's Own Corps of... ... 49
Gurkha Rifles (1st King George's Own) 49

Hackney (10th Lond. R.) 36
Hampshire Regiment, The 40
  „   „   6th Battalion 40
  „   „   7th Battalion 40
  „   „   8th Battalion 40
  „   Yeomanry 43
Herefordshire Regiment 34
Hertfordshire, Bedfordshire and, Regiment ... 21
  „   Regiment 34
Highland Light Infantry, 9th Battalion 34
  „   „   of Canada 53
Highlanders, Argyll and Sutherland 32
  „   Cameron 32
  „   Cape Town... 55
  „   Canada, Royal of 53
  „   Glasgow Regiment H.L.I. ... 31
  „   Gordon 31
  „   Royal (Black Watch) 27
  „   Seaforth 13
  „   5th Battalion 41
Honourable Artillery Company 14
Horse Guards, Royal 8
Hull, Le Regiment de (Canada) 53
Hussars, 3rd (The King's Own) 10
  „   4th (Queen's Own) 10
  „   7th (Queen's Own) 10
  „   8th (King's Royal Irish) 11
  „   10th Royal (Prince of Wales's Own) ... 11
  „   11th (Prince Albert's Own) 11
  „   13th/18th Royal... 12
  „   14th/20th 12
  „   15th (The King's Royal) 12

India (3rd Cavalry) 49
Infanterie de Joliette 52
Infantry, Light Durban 55
  „   Light Rand 55
Inniskilling Dragoon Guards (5th,) Royal ... 9
  „   Fusiliers, Royal 23
Inns of Court Regiment, The 39
Instructional Corps, S.A. 56
Irish Fusiliers, Royal 32
  „   Guards 16
  „   Hussars, King's Royal (8th) 11
Isle of Wight Rifles 40

Joliette, Infanterie de 52

Kensington Regiment 36
Kimberley Regiment 55
King Edward's Own Probyn's Horse (5th) ... 49

King's Dragoon Guards (1st) 8
„ Regiment (Liverpool) 19
„ Own Hussars (3rd) 10
„ „ Malta Regiment 39
„ „ Royal Regiment (Lancaster) 18
(Norf. Yeomanry) 44
„ „ Scottish Borderers 23
„ „ Yorkshire Light Infantry ... 29
„ Royal Hussars (15th) 12
„ „ Irish Hussars (8th) ... 11
„ „ Rifle Corps... 29
„ Shropshire Light Infantry 29

Lanarkshire Yeomanry 43
Lancashire Fusiliers 21
Lancaster (King's Own Royal Regiment) 18
„ York and, Regiment 30
Lancaster's, Duke of, Own Yeomanry ... 43
Lancers, 9th (Queen's Royal) 11
„ 12th Royal (Prince of Wales's) 12
„ 16th/5th 13
„ 17th/21st 13
Leicestershire Regiment 21
„ Yeomanry 42
Life Guards 8
Lincoln Regiment, The 51
Lincolnshire Regiment 19
Liverpool (The King's Regiment) ... 19
London, City of, Regiment 18
„ see pages 35, 36, 37, 38, 39
„ Irish Rifles 37
„ Rifle Brigade 35
„ Scottish 37
Lord Strathcona's Horse, Royal Canadians 51
Louw Wepener Regiment 54
Lovat's Scouts 34
Lothian & Border Yeomanry 45
Loyal Regiment (N. Lancashire) 28

Machine Gun Corps, Canadian 52
„ „ Squadron, S.A. 54
Madras Pioneers (1st) 49
Malaun Regiment 49
Malta Artillery (Royal) 14
„ Regiment (King's Own) 39
Manchester Regiment 30
Manitoba Dragoons, 12th 53
Marines, Royal 5
„ „ Emblems of Rank 7
Maisonneuve de, Regiment Le 52
Mechanised Transport Training Corps ... 59
Medical Corps, Royal Army 33
„ „ Royal Canadian Army ... 51
„ „ S.A. 56
Merchant Navy (Cap Badge) 5
Metropolitan Police 58
Middlesex Regiment 29
Military College, Royal, Sandhurst ... 46
„ Police, S.A., Corps of 56
„ Pioneer Corps, Auxiliary ... 46
Monmouthshire Regiment 25
„ „ (1st Battalion) 34
Montreal, Royal Regiment 52

Natal District Rifle Association 55
„ Mounted Rifles 56
„ Royal Carabiniers 56
Naval Service, Women's Royal 5

Navy, Army & Air Force Institutes 59
„ Merchant (Cap Badge) 5
„ Royal (Officers' Cap Badge) ... 5
„ Royal, Emblems of Rank 6
Norfolk Regiment, The Royal 19
„ Yeomanry 44
North Lancashire Loyal Regiment ... 28
„ Somerset Yeomanry 42
„ Staffordshire Regiment 30
Northamptonshire Regiment 28
„ Yeomanry, The 45
Northumberland Fusiliers 18
„ Hussars (Yeo.) 43
Nottinghamshire Yeomanry (Sherwood Raners) 41
Notts. and Derbys. Regiment 27
Nursing Sisters, Queen Alexandra's ... 59

Ordnance Corps, Royal Army 33
„ „ Royal Canadian 51
„ „ S.A. 56
Oxfordshire and Bucks. Light Infantry ... 27-39
„ Hussars, Queen's Own 45

Pay Corps, Royal Army 46
„ „ S.A. 55
Pioneer Corps, Auxiliary Military 46
Post Office Rifles (7th City of Lond. R.) ... 35
President Steyn Regiment 56
Pretoria Regiment (Princess Alice's Own) ... 54
Prince Albert's Own Hussars (11th) 11
„ „ (Leic. Yeo.) 42
„ „ (Somerset L.I.) 20
„ Albert Victor's Own 49
„ Alfred's Guard 54
Prince of Wales's 3rd Canadian Dragoons ... 53
„ „ Dragoon Guards (3rd) ... 9
„ „ (N. Stafford R.) 30
„ „ Own Royal Hussars (10th) ... 11
„ „ (R. Wilts. Yeo.) ... 13
„ „ (W. York R.) ... 20
„ „ (W. York R.) (7th/8th Battalion) 41
„ „ Royal Lancers (12th) 12
„ „ Own Scinde Horse 49
„ „ Vols. 26
Princess Beatrice's Isle of Wight Rifles... ... 40
„ Charlotte of Wales's (R. Berks. R.) ... 28
„ Louise Dragoon Guards 53
„ Louise's (A. & S.H.) 32
„ „ Kensington Regiment ... 36
„ Patricia's Canadian Light Infantry ... 53
Princess of Wales's Own Alexandra, York R. ... 21
„ Victoria's (R.I. Fus.) 32
Probyn's Horse (5th), King Edward's Own ... 49
Punjab Regiment (1st) 49
„ „ (8th) 49
„ „ (15th) 49

Queen Alexandra's Imperial Military Nursing Service 59
Queen Alexandra's R.N. Nursing Sisters ... 59
Queen Victoria's Rifles (9th Lond. R.) 35
Queen's Bays (2nd D.G.) 8
„ Own Cameron Highlanders 32
„ „ Dorset Yeomanry 43
„ „ Hussars (4th) 10
„ „ (7th) 10
„ „ (20th Lond. R.) 38

Queen's Own Oxford Hussars 45
„ „ Royal Regiment 41
„ „ „ West Kent Regiment ... 28
„ „ Worcester Hussars 44
„ „ Yorks. Dragoons 42
„ „ Rangers (1st Americans) 52
„ „ Royal Lancers (9th) 11
„ „ „ Regiment (West Surrey)... 17
„ „ Westminster and Civil Service Rifles ... 37

Rand Light Infantry 55
Rangers (12th Lond. R.) 36
Red Cross Society, British 59
Rifle Association, Natal District 55
„ Brigade 15
„ Corps (King's Royal) 29
Rifles (20th), Burma 49
„ Cape Peninsular 55
„ Mounted District 54
„ Witwatersrand 55
„ Natal Mounted 56
„ Umvoti Mounted 56
Robin Hood's Battalion Sherwood Foresters, The 40
Ross-shire Buffs (Seaforth Highrs.) 13
Royal Regiment (The Royal Scots) 17

St. John Ambulance Brigade, The 59
St. Pancras (19th Lond. R.) 38
S.A. Army Service Corps 56
„ Air Force 55
„ Artillery Regiment 55
„ Cadets 54
„ Corps of Military Police 56
„ Engineer Corps 56
„ General Officers 54
„ Instructional Corps 56
„ Machine Gun Squadron 54
„ Medical Corps 56
„ Ordnance Corps 56
„ Pay Corps 55
„ Special Service Battalions 54
„ Signals Corps 55
„ Veterinary Corps 55
Sandhurst, Royal Military College 46
Scinde Horse (14th) Prince of Wales's Own ... 49
Scots Fusiliers, Royal 22
„ Greys, Royal (2nd Dragoons) ... 10
„ Guards 16
„ Royal (The Royal Regiment) ... 17
Scottish, Canadian... 52
„ Horse Scouts 34
„ Borderers (King's Own) ... 23
„ Rifles (The Cameronians) ... 23
„ Transvaal, Regiment 54
Scouts, Lovat's (Terr. Army) 34
Seaforth Highlanders 13
„ 5th Battalion 41
Service Corps, R. Army 33
„ „ R. South Africa 56
„ „ R. Canadian 52
Sherwood Foresters (Notts. and Derbys. R.) ... 27
„ Rangers (Notts. Yeo.) ... 41
Shropshire Light Infantry (The King's) ... 29
„ Yeomanry 42
Signals, Royal Corps of 15
„ Royal Canadian Corps of ... 51
Somerset Light Infantry (Prince Albert's) ... 20

South Lancashire (Prince of Wales's Volunteers) 6
„ Notts Hussars 4
„ Staffordshire Regiment 2
„ Wales Borderers 4
„ „ (Brecknockshire Bn.) ... 5
„ Western District Regiment 5
Special Constabulary (Met.) 5
Special Service Battalion, S.A. 5
Staffordshire Yeomanry 3
„ Hussars 2
Suffolk Regiment 1
„ Hussars 4
Surrey Rifles (21st Lond. R.) 3
Sussex Regiment, Royal 2
„ „ (5th Bn. Cinque Ports) 2
Sutherland, Argyll and, Highlanders 3

Tank Regiment, Royal 1
Toronto Regiment (3rd) 5
Tower Hamlets Rifles (17th Lond. R.) ... 3
Transport Mechanised Training Corps 5
Transvaal Scottish Regiment 5

Ulster Rifles, Royal 2
Umvoti Mounted Rifles 5

Veterinary Corps, Canadian Army 5
„ „ Royal Army 3
„ „ S.A. 5

Warwickshire Regiment, Royal 1
„ Yeomanry 4
Welch Fusiliers, Royal 2
„ Regiment, The 2
Welsh Guards 1
Wentworth Regiment, The 5
Western Province Regiment 5
West Kent Regiment 2
„ Riding Regiment 2
„ Surrey 1
„ Yorkshire Regiment (The Prince of
Wales's Own) 20
„ „ „ (7th/8th Bn. of
Prince of Wales's Own) 4
Westminster and Civil Service Rifles 3
Weyburn Regiment, The 5
Wiltshire Regiment, The 30
„ Yeomanry 1
Witwatersrand Rifles 5
Women's Auxiliary Air Force 4
„ „ Territorial Service 59
„ Royal Naval Service ...
„ Legion, The 5
„ Land Army 5
„ Transport Service (F.A.N.Y.) ... 5
„ Volunteer Service 5
Worcestershire Regiment 2
„ Hussars, Queen's Own ... 4

York a d Lancaster Regiment 3
Yorkshire Dragoons, Yeomanry 4
„ Hussars, Yeomanry 2
„ Light Infantry, King's Own ... 2
„ Regiment (Green Howards) ... 2
Yorkton Regiment 5